ACORNS AND ABALONE

2017

Sylvia Ross
aka Stephenson Ross

check out the story
on p. 63 – even if
you don't like
poetry. ♡

ACORNS AND ABALONE
a collection of poems, drawings and short stories

Copyright 1968 - 2017 Sylvia Ross
ISBN: 978-0-615-52721-5   Bentley Avenue Books

I wish to thank the following publishers, editors, and exhibiters who have helped my work come to the attention of the public: the late Omar Salinas of the Fresno State College Association's magazine *Backwash*; Margaret Dubin and Lindsie Bear, *News from Native California Quarterly Magazine*; Malcolm Margolin, publisher, and editors Jeannine Gendar and Gayle Wattawa of Heyday, Berkeley, California who assisted with my earlier books; John Dofflemyer, poet as well as publisher, of *Dry Crik Journal*, Lemon Cove, California; CERA; The Kings -Tulare Arts Council; Arts Visalia; The Kaweah Land Arts Festival; The Bay Area Poets' Coalition. I also thank the many museums, libraries, and organizations that have supported my work and that of many other California writers, and in particular, the Porterville Historical Museum, Three Rivers Historical Museum, Tulare County Historical Museum, and the Tule River Indian Reservation, Visalia Chapter, DAR, Eta Zeta Chapter, DKG.

Previously published works credited pages 116 through 118.

Orders, inquiries, and correspondence for **Lion Singer** and **Blue Jay Girl** should be should be addressed to: Heyday Books P.O. Box 9145 Berkeley, CA 94709, (510) 549-3564, Fax (510) 549-1889 heyday@heydaybooks.com

ACORNS AND ABALONE

by
Sylvia Ross

2017

Table of Contents

PART I: <u>Acorns and Abalone</u>

PART II: <u>Out of Sandy Loam and Red Clay</u>

PART III: <u>Some Stories, old and new</u>

~addenda~

dedicated to my husband,
our sons,
the daughters they brought to us
and the children
that followed

PART I: *Acorns and Abalone*

...any kind of pagan sign will do"

"February"
Dry Crik Journal 2013
John Dofflemyer

Oak Trees

While poets talked, oak trees grew
Beneath their feet, grew strong branches
To hold up skies, grew strong roots
To crack roads, grew shiny leaves
To drift into the cracks.
While poets talked, oak trees grew
Beneath their feet, made mats of twigs
To house small spiders, opened up spaces
To pairing birds, grew rich acorns
To feed hungry ghost people.
While poets talked, grasses sprouted,
Lichens spread across granite outcrops.
Generations of herd animals grazed
And seedlings grew into forests
While poets talked.

(for Salinas, Mezey, Ginsberg, Dofflemyer, and Hernandez)

9

Roundelay for Ghost Singers

In the night most part of winter
When the fog drips wet and cold
Shadows weave beyond the fire
Sweet smoke calls forth old voices
Children hear ancient stories

When the fog drips wet and cold
Shadows weave beyond the fire
Sweet smoke calls forth old voices
Children hear ancient stories
In the night most part of winter

Shadows weave beyond the fire
Sweet smoke calls forth old voices
Children hear ancient stories
In the night most part of winter
When the fog drips wet and cold

Sweet smoke calls forth old voices
Children hear ancient stories
In the night most part of winter
When the fog drips wet and cold
Shadows weave beyond the fire

Children hear ancient stories
In the night most part of winter
When the fog drips wet and cold
Shadows weave beyond the fire
Sweet smoke calls forth old voices

Art Theft

Mary sits front row in drawing class. She's vain
of her tattoo. Its color and intricacy
impresses but gives little
competition
to the grandeur of the darkly
twisted braid that teases my eyes.
My envious pencil makes her beauty my own.

(for Mary)

The Seagulls' Banquet

fragments of shell whitening on the beach,
traces of the fragging of one organism
by another

beauty emerges from destruction
a dawn walk's reminder that
living things survive only by interference
with the survival of other living things

so, looking for small kindnesses,
soft voices, a repudiation
of harsh and unwanted knowledge

I welcome denial that I am both abalone
and hungry gull, and hold back witness
that a broken shell is no more
beautiful than a beach sand feather.

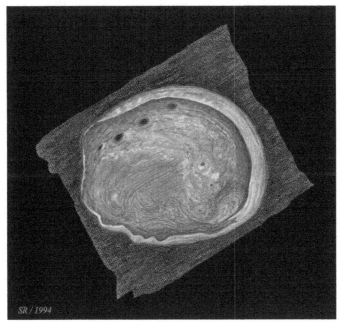

Ted's abalone shell prismacolor drawing, an exercise in photo-realistic rendering

13

Conversation

In the sun in the patio at the seniors,
we got our handwork out.
She's starting something.
She don't know what.
Our fingers keep workin'.
I hook these little squares.
They like them down at the church.
Those girls there
sew them together for babies
over in Arizona.
Her blue eyes look right at me
an' she asks if Shawna makes
baskets. I say no. She says,
"You know how to make them,
so why doncha teach her?
Shame how your people are giving up
on all those things you used to know.
Shawna don't want to make baskets.
She got a job now down there
at the Fried Chicken, making good money.
But I don't say nothing.
Our fingers move and the sun moves.
It comes warm 'round our backs.
Looks like she's going
to do something now.
Those two needles begin to make a song.
She asks for some of my yarn
and I give it to her. An' by our feet,
the box fills up with bright patches.
Her granddaughter Denine works down
at the Taco Bell since summer.
I ask her if Denine knows how
to knit them fine fishermen sweaters.
She says kids today just don't
want to learn nothing what takes time.

14

Tribal Identity Grade Three

The recess bell rings and we rush
for the hopscotch game
before the fourth grade is out.

Sister talked about the Plains Indians.
We saw a film on Navajos.
We colored a ditto of a pueblo.

Lisa brags, "I'm part Indian.
I'm Cherokee." She flips her blonde
curls and her feet own the ground.

"Me too," I say. "I'm part Indian too."
"Well, what are you then?" she asks.
"I'm Chik Chancy," I answer.

"That's not a tribe," she tells the girls
They turn away laughing.
"It is." I tell them. But they don't hear.

The clip hits the sixth square
and then richochets out past the line.
I pick it up and put it back.

Chik Chancy is a tribe.

Cultural Capitulation

Below the cold white sun and swooping crows,
skaggy branches reach for my old red truck.
I like the truck's bright color. Maybe the trees do too.
The grey trees long ago pushed past fence lines.
Brooms of eucalyptus branches scrape the windows.
Leaves block any view of the easement road.
I drive on and don't see a snake,
but the truck's wheels bump twice over its length.
In the mirror - the banded snake lies in the ruts, dead,
only fit for the crows - I brake the truck too late.
It's time to evict these damned foreign trees.
I can't worry whose property they're on. Not mine.
Oak belongs here. Eucalyptus doesn't.
I have saw and shears and axe,
could strip this foreign arboretum to the ground,
take revenge on its trees
for my accidental killing of a snake.
The intrepid crows, longer residents of this valley
than any of my own indigenous ancients,
wheel in the air. They squawk and scold at my intent.
Crows live in these dubious trees, nest, adapt.
It's time to go home, to the sofa, to a cup
of imported coffee, to a consideration of snakes,
Australian trees, and the essential dominance
of crows.

Crow and Raven

Ahduhwut soars in the canyons of Gawea
with his brothers
his sisters
his children
Ahduhwut nests in the canyons of Gawea
with his brothers
his sisters
his children
Ahduhwut laughs in the canyons of Gawea
with his brothers
his sisters
his children
Ahduhwut, invincible,
takes what he wants

TISA MUY ~ Spring

In the time of energy, *tisa muy*
When water from the cold rains
Finally sinks down through dead leaves,
The spirits of the earth beneath
Our world begin to dance.
Under sand, humus and clay, under
The racing water of rivers,
They shake gourds of rock and
Rattles of stone; make flutes of
Hollow dead roots.

In the time of energy, tisa muy,
The spirits of the earth make a dance
Down in that dark world
Until waste acorns grow leaves to free

Themselves from the clanging racket
Of the soil---until the wise little green
Grasses climb from the darkness
To a place of safety. Every day higher
Those things climb to get away
From the dancing of the earth's spirits.
Higher into the air and light of the sun
They climb.

In the time of energy, *tisa muy*,
The spirits of the earth
Show no kindness.

(in memory of Rosanna Ramos)

Letter from an Indian Graveyard

Little sister,
The children are hunting obsidian
and we are resting and watching
the last of winter.

I hear the Chukchansi woman
who came down from these Auberry hills
to the pony station by the river.
the green barley has hidden her,
but she is whispering in the new grass
and she has the voice of
your gentle savagery.

Little sister, ancestor,
how does a voice of wild barley taste?

19

Cowboys and Indians

My mom said her grandmother
Loved the cowboy's blue eyes
And he loved her low voice
And shy ways
And he'd never known
A woman who could skin
A rabbit so fast.
Then her mother in turn
Found another cowboy
 With blue eyes.
So we ended up pale.
One of my brothers even has
Blue cowboy eyes.
I'm a dark-haired woman
With a low voice
And shy ways
Like all those women
Before me.
I don't know if I could skin
A rabbit so fast.
I don't know if
I could skin a rabbit.
I think I could.

Hayalu Yate Yenana
- the caretaker -

The air has no breeze and heat has no sound. The
woman can't hear the waves that shimmer in the air
above her path. Summer is a quiet season.
Burdened with deer hide flasks, her digging stick, a
sleeping baby, she follows a tiny dry waterway up
the hill from the even drier bed of a stony, dusty
river. Sweating, and tired from the walk to find
water, she leans against a big tree. It's sticky on her
shoulder. She finds honey. And, down beneath the
tree, a small pool of clean water.

She gathers gifts for the elders and the sick left
behind when the people of Apasau went up into the
pines for a cooler camp. The sounds of summer are
around her: a buzzing rattle of bees and a slowly
piping stream, the drumbeat that comes from her
own body. Summer music.

The shrill caw of a blue jay sounds, then the
switching of a lizard's tail. Above her, a sere and
brown leaf falls but makes no noise. Summer
welcomes silence. *Hayalu Yate Yenana.*

21

The Hillwife's Kitchen

It wasn't so much
That she minded rowdiness
The grab-ass revelry
The plate breaking
Milk spilling
Loud and careless
Counter bashing
Rambunctiousness
That came when they all
Happened to be home
At the same time
Or that she preferred
The empty sink quiet
Of so much of the rest
Of her year
But the draggy solitude
filled days
Orderly and scrubbed
Stretched out her time
Like hands pulling
At taffy or
Kneading dough
And this homecoming
Crowded her
With great rib crushing hugs
Iron skillet wit
Laughing profanities
Apron snagging humor
And endless cooking
It reminded her
How some meals
Hard to prepare
Can be too quickly eaten

Sister Mary Immaculata modeled for Vermeer

Salem '68

that night when
we first saw that the man
in the moon
has a slavic woman's face
and we went
running after
to ask why the slavic women
who had always been
so merry
made keening sounds at
my wedding

that night when i became
a green flaming witch
and you
a slightly phallic broom
and we went hunting
the black boots and red
fringed shawl
of the moon

we found loud balalikas
playing
among constellations
and we forgot
to ask

Bondage Games

Desperate now, and clever
with the slyness
of other mute women
like chained dogs, hobbled beasts,
I twist my head and writhing
try to break free.
Pulling back, recklessly then
surge forward,
but he holds me tethered
by soft mouth, pale eyes.

I am as tightly collared
on the leash of his displeasure
as he is chained to the
taunting lead of mine.
These tortured movements
give violent celebration
to each's own cruel option.

Sisters

Talking in the kitchen until late
When everyone else is asleep
Sister we are the bear women.
We wear abalone necklaces.
We carry baskets.
We hold our men in great bear women
Arms.
Sister, we were too far apart
In our births.
We never played together,
Never danced with the same boys,
Didn't share small children
Like other sisters did.
 But while you talk
Our mother's voice comes out of
Your wonderful bear woman mouth.
Our mother's laugh shakes your belly,
Though it is much smaller
Than hers ever was.
My sister we are the bear women.
We have the power
To crash through brush, to smash
The clouds and pluck down stars
And make a meal.
Sister, tonight your voice
Brings our mother back to us.
Her great bear woman presence
Fills all the space
Of this room.

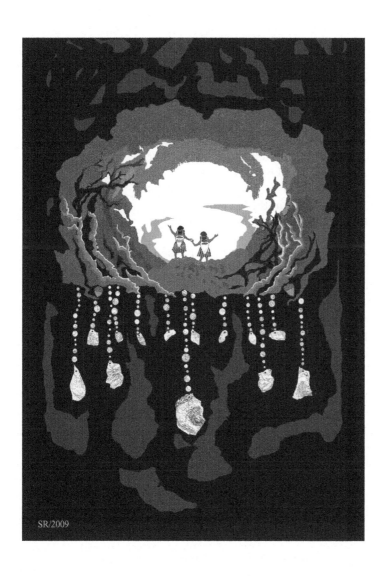

Marge's Shoes

The first few years she wore them
I didn't even notice the leather's soft tan,
and buckskin laces roughly looped.
By the time I paid attention, her feet
had already curved the shoes inward,
weather had toughened the soft leather,
and one lace had broken short.
Then I asked where she got those shoes
and she said from the Indian store
down in Mountain View.

Some other time, another year, I asked
the name of the Indian store
that sold handmade shoes like hers,
but she said it went out of business
and no store sold mocs with vodka
splatters and Yosemite dirt ground in
with a little tamale pie, so I couldn't
buy shoes like hers anyway.

Last summer, laughing and crying
together, in the campground
at Lake Mendocino, on the night
before her youngest son's wedding
while the men drank beer and talked of
politics and sports,
I told her how much I really, really liked
those old shoes of hers. So
she took them off and gave them to me.

These beat-up, raggedy Kaibab moccasins
I wear are stained and worn rough
by hard years in my friend's life.
I wear them when I need her courage.

Helen's Raggedies

SR/1996

The Birthday Party

They grow up around me like party balloons
with wild laughing faces and come to
my knees and thighs and waist and shoulders
for a little while and then sail away
all smiling and many-colored
and their eyes
never looked at me anyway
Then I think about Gefion
who hungered for power
So that some old god promised her all the land
she could plow in a night
and she turned her sons in to oxen
and plowed a plot the size of Denmark
and he had to give it to her
It is a funny story and I get
hungry too
So I think I'll turn mine into bulls
and they can seed the San Joaquin Valley
It'll be mine then
O I'm happy
But what happens when they outgrow parties
I watch the plastic bayonets
of these mocking children
their bellies fat with cake
and find myself reaching for bits
of broken color

Grandpa's Beard

Admonition

Don't give up touch, grandchildren.
feel beards, beads, fabrics, fibers, hair, reeds,
skin, yarns, piano keys, strings, soil, smooth stone.
Take delight in whatever intrigues your fingers.
e.e. cummings was right, and
"...feeling is first..."

31

Matrilineage

The only picture I have
Of my great-grandmother
Shows her lying
In her coffin.
No one thought to take
A picture of the Chukchansi
Woman
Until time had passed away.

The best picture I have
Of my grandmother
Shows her holding
Her sister's stillborn boy
He was a fat and beautiful baby.
She looks down at him.
Seems like no one
In my family
Thinks about time
Until it's gone.

I have lots and lots
Of pictures of my mother, but
None show her
Standing in a kitchen,

Apron stretched
Across her fat belly,
Dimples winking
From her round cheeks
As she tells some truth
Funnier than lies.

Laughing 1988

33

Haswana Wotiye
(a dance for the dead)

In ancient days, Chukchansi cremated their dead
Old history's words both in dry phrase
And condescending journal entry gives record.
The dead one's band would kindle a huge fire
And host a nightlong dance. Drums and deer hooves'
Rattling pulse gave furious mourning to the dead
As women would circle and begin to dance. Around
And around the pyre, ever quicker around, they'd spin
In frenzied cadence to fire, to the night, to loss.
Cinders springing from fire to dancers
Would singe the women's hair, blacken their faces
While dust and sweat from the violence of grieving
Joined with smoke and the color of flame
To carry the dead one's body away from the earth,
Body gone to find death-stolen spirit.
Then, when flames had morphed to cool grey ash and
Fragments of bone, our ancients in honoring tradition
Would never speak the name of the dead again
When I die don't cry or wail, don't grieve.
Don't host a dance for me. Just sew my ashes
Into your mattress to soften your sleep
Where, selfish and vicious as any old witch woman,
I'll warily keep watch through all your nights
And will slip into the erotic arcady of your drowsing
Filling it so full of memory you'll weep joyous dreams
And awaken so contentedly from the night
That you'll want no other woman.

Haswana Wotiye, con't.

But sweet one, if you should die before me
Leaving me in this sterile and too civilized world,
Where satin pillows and pious prayers are given the dead
In quiet rooms that give no welcome to the old gods
Or to me, I'll go out and find a wild, natural place
And build a fiery mound on raw and rocky dirt.
I'll throw my love for you into the kindle
Of sticks, the broken branches of native trees, and
Dry vines gathered as the whips of my sorrow.
I'll shriek and wail around that fire until I have no voice.
I'll dance for you until my naked feet are cracked
And blistered, around and around until in a furied rhythm
The flames themselves come to dance with me.
Spinning around that climbing, growling circle of fire
Until the ashes of mourning are all that is left of its flame,
I'll dance and dance until my spirit follows yours,
Until the dance is broken to such silence
That never again will I say your name.

***

Vertebral Doggerel

Would it be so difficult to cope
with being an ant?
It might be nice to be
an ant or roach or scorpion,
often social, ever industrious.
One might hope
thoughts more relevant
would arise from neurons safely
inside an exoskeleton,
that ideas, grand and illustrious,
would find the firing there superior
unimpeded by a bony interior.

SR/1992

coital conjunction
a gathering of rude weeds
and a cobalt vase

Handwork

our hands
tell the story
of
every woman
who
came
before us
and
everything
we
cook
clean
love
find abandoned
and
reclaim
with
our touch is
held in ancient hands
as
our voices
sing the songs
sung
by
all the women
inside
us

We still wear tattoos
We still wear tattoos
We still wear tattoos
We still wear tattoos
We still wear tattoos
We still wear tattoos

~~~<O>~~~

PART II: *Out of Sandy Loam and Red Clay*

~~~<O>~~~

The Day of Pagan Sign

in the morning seven acorns
littered the ground
a constellation's pattern

roadrunner's repeated
pacing below the barbed wire
kept a red-tail away

just across the driveway
during the sleepy afternoon
a bobcat posed watching

wildfire smoke raging
against the setting sun
drifted black against red

coyote's moon rose luminous
it gives no sleep
only dangerous dreams

the mesquite's shadow
on a coyote's moonlit path
carries real thorns

Nancy's Pink Hat

I'd bought a silky beige hat to go with the beige
Summer suit, white bag, skinny stiletto heels.
It was a small, veiled pillbox, Grace Kelly style.

My sister scowled and brought me her pink hat,
The one she'd worn Easter, at the May Festival,
And mass on Sundays since. Not new, or veiled,
Or silky. It didn't match the beige summer suit.

But my sister was usually right about that kind
Of thing. The hat was the prettier for being hers,
On the day I ran away with a blue-eyed man.

44

1957 "Going Away"

45

Reparation

my mother-in-law's
small even stitches mended
more than torn fabric

an elegant patch
where kind words sewn would soften
another's cruel

her sewing basket
with pins scattered out of place
waits for diligence

the fraying wicker
coaxes my complicity
in making repairs

Frazier Valley

no ranch house
geraniums
in coffee cans
on the porch rail
here.
no garden
with beans
and tomatoes.
no grapevines
gone wild.

cattle gone
with the milk cow,
the hog pen,
plow, scraper,
hand hoes,
shovels, sheds,
the barn.

scrub grasses
and a derelict
pair
wait it out
hoping
for rain
and conversing

during their
solitary
survivorship

for Ellen and Ben

Under Coyote's Moon

Words expended
in the canyons of gender, all nesting places erased,
no fragrant earth, no streaming crashing rivers,
no silky reeds to wave a warm breath greeting.

Voices stilled
where sounds are muted, whispered repetitions lost.
no songs audible, not a sub-sound vibrates the air,
nothing left sparks a tinder of warmth or welcome.

Senses hardened
to calcification, the non-comfort of stick-like bones.
fingertips' ridges, dulled and time-worn smooth,
grasp to reclaim what fragments memory retains.

Awarenesses fused
a slight touch ignites conjoined sensate humming,
torches life to uncompromised remembrances,
across time mirroring infinities spin out a dance.

kintsukori: the Japanese art of using gold or other metals in
the mending of broken crockery

Kintsukori

a precious repair
this small and humble vessel
hallows redemption

Cannibal Thoughts

In quiet classrooms stealthy lice nibble
the detritus of children's scalps.
In his medical office, a gynecologist listens
while a patient complains
of vaginal fungus.
In the elevator a well groomed man
rubbed an ear where a tiny mite was nesting.

Smugly, in the sunny patio near me,
a sculptured girl glances around,
loudly presents a complicated vegan order.
The harried, disinterested waiter
serving our tables sighs.
But, I appreciate how she asserts
the righteousness of her conscience.

Yet the incisors in my mouth are designed
to rip, shred and tear this chop
positioned on my plate looking tender and
pleasingly prepared. Overdosing on
biologic certainties,
I listen as she proclaims her concerns.
Time's tutelage gives us many sympathies.

I'm sensitive to her youthful assurance.
But the gods of perversity
ordained this planet to their choosing.
In her first pregnancy the disdainful girl
at the table next to mine
will likely suffer through craving
the very foods she proudly denies today.

A mosquito interrupts this patio rumination.
I pause the arc of my fork
to feel loathing, not for stockyard butchers,
bistro chefs, or my fellow omnivores,
but for those annoying gods
who chose to set out life forms
who thrive best when feasting on each other.

***

Kitchen Observation

citrus
past its prime
a self-portrait of sorts
still useable through its rind
by an imaginative cook
although its general usefulness
has much diminished
with time.

old lemons

Shapeshifters

The gods of adversity,
for once in accord, decided to mold
a gigantic towering sculpture,
one solitary mountain,
that would tease the much too grand Sierra
on the east and taunt the punier Coast Range
equidistant to the west.
The gods thought to improve
on feldspar and granite,
so they combined sandy loam
with red clay, poured in sweet river water.
The doughy mix in their rough old hands
felt so soft and pleasant
as they kneaded and shaped the grog
they felt themselves shrink and grow breasts
and soft fat arms. They became goddesses
and giggled and told stories,
shared gossip about the other goddesses
(as women grinding acorns,
making tamales,
or setting a church potluck might do.)
And when the gods finished
messing up California's kitchen, dirtying
its alluvial floor,
being women they changed their minds
about making a mountain.
And just for the fun of it (as children might do)
they patted the mountain down pancake flat
to cover the wide valley floor,
where they left the hardpan marks of their fingers
to repulse both shovel and posthole digger,
to wreck a rich man's dozer
as easily as a poor man's plow.
then, with a full day's artistryfinished,
went home to their wives.

54

Barefoot and Pregnant
(a counter-cultural confession)

"barefoot and pregnant"
odious words
no girl wanted to be
a grunged source of shame,
chattel, a drudge, a slavey
to diapers drying
in the living room
more babies than one
splashing in the bath
soup bones boiling in a pot
my harried love rushing back
to a needed second job
scarcely greeted or fed
floors to wash, ironing to do
little comfort and less money
but still when I, in maudlin
and sentimental mood,
reflect on my
best and happiest time
I go back to days when
I was that girl
barefoot and pregnant

The Hawk

she envied the flight of hawks, the soaring birds
she listened to them screaming their avian words
as she worked beyond the barn and pasture.
their screeching freedom helped her endure
broodish days. she was too tightly earth-bound
and imagined the hawks screamed her own sound
brash and wild. but she hoed dry season weeds
and cleared her mind by choosing which seeds
she'd plant in this arid patch beyond the corral,
a section neglected, non-productive, non-fertile.

her work's reclamation of this barren, harsh,
desert land's equivalent of a wet lands marsh
gave her a place where whimsy could be sown,
a plot of sunflowers, daisies, a garden her own.
her hands set a cadence with the hoe's drop,
a rhythmical dull whack, until in an abrupt stop--
so close to the blade, down in slinking briars
long twined with ancient rusted fence wire,
a harrier, its leg bound by the bloody wrap
of its lured kill caught in a cruelly accidental trap

of metal strands and creeping vines hugging
the hawk to earth. In the bird's frantic tugging
the harrier's sharp beak was opening and closing,
opening, closing; and she, vainly supposing
herself capable, and poised so near,
the woman chose to try to pull the hawk clear.
she was coop-familiar, stealthy catching a hen,
or subduing a rooster, she dropped the hoe, then
pounced. but it fought her. massive wings beat

56

wide. she twisted, kept hold, swerved, her feet
off balance, the woman pitched forward, squat
down gracelessly, aware that she was caught.

And, scared now, moved with quickened actions
to evade the bird's angry beak, its wicked talons.
the hawk couldn't know her impulsive motive,
how she intended the bird turned free to live,
to fly, and how unable to loft the hawk skyward,
or let it go, she too was trapped. in fear, she heard
a reedy high-pitched music screaming out
filling the air, the shrill piercing noise of a shout
going beyond the barn, a cry sent reaching
to the sky - her own voice - a hawk's screeching.

***

Desktop Stalker

my conflicted fingers key
to remembered streets,
the numbers of past places
fromone, my silent mother
watched cars below
while I roamed
knocking on doors.
we moved to another home
much better for her
harsh entrapment for me.
I key away to a windswept
Madera ranch where I was
cherished, told long
stories in the dry
soft shade past the pump,
a windmill squeaking,
a swing squeaking,
pipe smoke blending
with eucalyptus leaves
and the smell of dust.
a lonely old man sat
and shared his wife's
ghost with me
under a line of tall trees
she'd planted,ordered out
from San Francisco.
only the trees remain.
my fingers go clacking
their way across map grids
trying to find the house,
the barn, the chickens.

58

But this screen
lacks another universe—
an arc of needed dimension.
I rudely trek
through other people's
quiet todays, see my past
addresses, go wandering
through walled places,
a different California.
Palms, Culver City,
West L.A., Burlingame.
In freedom, I explore
Granada Hills, Burbank,
Inglewood, Oxnard,
Red Bluff. Then Fresno,
Porterville, Springville,
Exeter, tracing electronic
trail markers, the gift
of choice, to the places
of sweet education
the valley of cherishing.

this desktop stalking
has done no harm. merely
a geographic intrusion
into quiet landscapes
of other's eminent domain,
to beg humble inclusion
for the incipient ghost,
of this woman, who like
her unknown grandmother,
likes to plant trees.

Old Ladies' Lament

I've kept too much stuff, I have, I have.
My closets have dresses galore.
I don't go anywhere much these days,
I should chuck them out the back door.

I've kept too much stuff, I have, I have.
Books and pictures cover every wall.
People carry pictures in phones now.
Very few read actual books at all.

I've kept too much stuff, I have, I have,
Make-up, tubes of lotions, vitamins.
None of it bought me eternal youth.
My face shows the range of my sins.

I've kept too much stuff, I have, I have.
Receipts, letters, cards from my past.
Bank statements are up in the ether,
Only I believed paper would last.

I've kept too much stuff, I have, I have
I've kept too much stuff in this place.
My children don't want a bit of it,
Find my treasures a cultural disgrace.

I've kept too much stuff, I have, I have.
I'll bequeath it to a consignment mart.
I know all anyone honestly needs
Would tuck into a bag lady's cart.

PART III: *Short Stories*

~~~<O>~~~

The Significance of an Arched Door
a true story

In the spring of 1968, we lived in Fresno. My husband taught typing and bookkeeping at McLane High. We had four young sons and little money. Our house was small. The four boys slept in two sets of bunk beds in the bigger bedroom. My husband and I shared the smaller one. But the house had a big yard where Bob grew our vegetables year round.

I was going to school at night when my husband was home to take care of the children. I'd made an agreement with him. I wanted more children than his practical mind felt we could afford, so I'd promised to earn a degree and help him support a bigger than average family. Every extra penny of his salary went to pay for my books and tuition and to keep the boys in clothing and shoes. He taught at Fresno City College at night for extra money, but we had little for entertainment to give our children beyond TV and hikes in the Sierra.

It was a pretty spring following a dreary winter. The valley fog was gone, blossoms were out in the orchards and the sun was shining again. The *Fresno Bee* advertised that Roeding Park's Storyland had been at last been reopened after some long and lengthy repairs, and Bob decided that the boys and I needed a special treat.

So, on Sunday I fixed at a picnic lunch, and we went to the park. We went to the zoo first. Of all the wonders of the excellent collection of animals at the small city's zoo, the boys seemed to like the seals best. But their favorite zoo activity was just outside its gate. As we left, the boys took time to roll down a high grassy berm.

We found a table under trees and the older boys helped set out our picnic. Afterward, we walked through the grand arboretum that Roeding Park was, read the identification markers in front of specimen trees and to the boys' delight, went into Storyland.

The two-year-old was tired and in the baby-pack, snoozing on Bob's back. The older three boys ran ahead, delighted with what they found, racing from the area dedicated to Red Riding Hood through to a shady arbor to find the Three Little Pigs' houses. I followed after, as childishly gleeful as they were.

I grew tired of trying to keep up with the three boys. I went back to sit on the bench with Bob and the baby trying not to wake the little one. I remember putting a soft cloth diaper over our sleeping son's fair hair, lest he sunburn. It was peaceful sitting there, but the moment was interrupted when our three wide awake school boys ran back, grabbed my hands and pulled me away to see a discovery that they knew I'd like. I did like it. The place that they'd found was built on a path that curved high atop another park berm. It was a fairy tale princess's castle.

Our home in Fresno was far from ocean pier arcades with games or even a merry-go-round. The boys were naïve enough to be enchanted by walls of manufactured stone and fake battlements. They had yet to visit Disneyland or Knott's Berry Farm. Magic Mountain, which would be closer to the great central valley, existed only on paper.

A castle in a valley park was wonder enough! I had seen amusement parks, more than once, but I too was enchanted.

The two older boys couldn't be contained long and morphed into medieval warriors storming the castle, thrusting imaginary spears and shooting imaginary arrows from the arched windows, shouting at each other. Our sons were soon joined by other children, and the castle's battlements filled with boys and girls lured and made captive by our boys' charm and wild energy improvising scenarios of knights and ladies — and sword fights.

I stayed in the castle's central room for a few minutes, looking down from its arched windows, and feeling like I was a princess in spite of having four children and a very busy life trying to match their liveliness, the house, and my studies. Our third son, kindergarten-aged, stayed with me. We were sharing a moment of quiet ignoring the blustering play going on around us. I knew he loved Storyland's architecture. He was a thoughtful child who liked to draw pictures and build Lincoln Log towers.

"Wouldn't it be fun to live in a castle?" I asked.

He paused before answering, then he slipped his small hand into mine. "When I grow up, I'll build a castle for you, Mom."

*

Many years passed. My husband and I grew old. By 2004, we had enjoyed good careers and were now retired. Our sons had degrees, families, and good jobs. We were proud of all of them. Our work was done. Our children had grown to adulthood, and they all had made us very proud. That third child, true to his nature, had taken departmental honors in Industrial Design at Fresno State.

He and our daughter-in-law had finished building a lovely home,that he designed and her contractor brothers

66

built on five acres in the foothills of the Sierra. The property had a beautiful view, and the two of them were now in the process of building a small house on their hilltop for my husband and me. It would be the place we'd live, near them, for the duration of our old age. The little house was almost finished. Our son was excited about something he had added to the plan and his brothers-in-law had worked to add to the house. He wanted us to come to the property to see it.

We were always eager to see the progress of the building where we would soon live. We drove over to see the new inclusion to the house. It was something that hadn't shown on the plans or carefully drafted elevation drawings. We were amazed that the most marvelous front door had been added to our almost finished cottage.

The grand door had been specially ordered, and it must have cost three times the price of any ordinary front door. Heavily planked, two inches thick and with an iron-gridded peephole window, the arched door welcomed any guest into an entirely different sort of world. It was the kind of front door that suited a castle.

Bob went on into the house, checking on the builders' finish work's progress, looking for stray nails or bits of wallboard to clean up. Our son and I stayed out on the front porch. I was unable to stop gazing in admiration at the unusual and specially ordered door.

Everything about the door pleased me. It was a most unusually heavy and magnificent door for a small cottage-sized house, and that very lack of synchrony pleased me too. For a long time, I couldn't say anything.

Through wet eyes, I looked up at the great, tall, quiet man beside me. Nathan now was thirty-six years past the once-upon-a-time we had stood together in Roeding Park's Storyland, wondering at the princess's castle. He had barely come up to my waist then.

"Do you remember that once you promised to build me a castle?" I softly asked him.
He put his arm around me, and he said, "I always remembered, Mom. I didn't know if you'd remembered."

***

Winter Beginning, Winter Ending

(Sarah Ellen's Story, 1919)

At the beginning of winter, 1919, when it was finally cold enough in the valley to keep meat hanging in the shed from spoiling too soon, a man named Ernie took it into his mind to go up into the hill country of Madera County to his wife's people. His plan was to get venison, even perhaps bear meat to season and smoke for winter. He favored elk, but the elk herds were already disappearing. He hadn't seen an elk in three years of trekking the Sierra with his wife's people.

Ernie liked his wife's relatives. Indian people didn't seem to mind the scarred face or the blind white eye he presented. They took him for what he did, not for how he looked. They were the truest people he knew. He packed bags of raisins the Italians down the road had given him to take up to Mrs. Billy. He knew she'd like that, and not mind Billy going off with him to hunt for a few days or a week. This year Sarah Ellen might get her first deer. That'd be better than elk or bear.

Ernie was a white man and his wife, Reenie, had been dead for nearly seven years. He'd promised her as she was dying that their daughter would know who she was. He kept his promise, and his daughter, Sarah Ellen, did know she was.

She knew her mother had been half Chukchansi, and she knew that her mother had been born in a place called Fresno Flats up in the hills.

Ernie told her that her mother had signed on as a harvest crew's cook in 1909, 1910 and 1911 to save the money to buy the forty acres where they lived and he had taken care of her when her mother was away.

The little girl knew that if her mother hadn't died, she have a little brother six or seven-years-old and a mother like everyone else. But she didn't remember them. She could only miss the idea of them. She didn't miss them.

The best part of her life was going up into the hill country. Ever since the little girl could remember, she had traveled in the buckboard with her dad up into the mountains six or eight times a year. She liked the long ride across the plains, and sleeping out under the night sky. Ernie would tell her of her mother and her grandmother. He told her most of the Indian people in the hills were her mother's relatives and therefore they were her relatives.

She thought very often of her Indian grandmother. Her grandmother had been dead long before she was born. But, she knew that her grandmother had been taken away from her tribe to be a worker on a ranch in Crane Valley when she was a tiny girl, and then when she was almost grown had run away from that mean ranch to the stage depot at Fort Miller where she got paid real wages for kitchen work. Sarah Ellen thought that was a very brave thing to do. She couldn't imagine running away from what she knew to what she didn't know.

She liked it when they went up by the reservoir that covered Crane Valley with water. Ernie told her that water had filled it up in 1912, that both Uncle Billy and Tom worked on the dam. She thought about what had happened to the ranches that used to be there. Were there still houses and barns and fences under the water? She wondered and wondered. The long wedge of blue water behind the dam taught her that everything changes and nothing ever stays the same.

Once she had a mother and now she didn't. Once there was a ranch where a stolen Indian child worked and now there was a shimmery lake. Once the digger Indians were naked savages. It said so in her schoolbooks. But now Uncle Billy wore plaid shirts and overalls just like her dad. She wondered if she were a digger Indian. She thought maybe she was.

She was never frightened of traveling up into the mountains. Her dad was always with her and everyone she met was good to her. She liked the old men who'd fish and hunt with them, her Indian family. There was only one woman she knew. Mrs. Billy. She never left her cabin, and didn't speak good English, but she was always

71

happy to see Sarah Ellen. Mrs. Billy called her 'Little Reenie' after her mother. But this trip was impulsive. She hadn't known it was coming.

She'd felt headachy walking home from school that Wednesday in early December and thought she would lie down on her cot until time for supper. But when she came to their lane Ernie was busy loading up the wagon with supplies. A barrel of stock grain and two cans of kerosene were in the bed of the wagon, and her dad was lifting the heavy canvas tent over its side. She didn't feel her usual excitement. She didn't feel really good.

Besides, she was in fifth grade now and didn't want to miss school. Teacher didn't like it when she was absent. Her dad had given her a big smile when he saw her come up the lane through the fog. He told her to get her bedroll ready, oil her snake boots and get her warm mountain gear. He reminded her that there might be snow if they'd need to climb 'way high to get to a good spot to find deer and bear.

She told him that teacher wanted her in class, and he made a face at her. "I don't want to skip," she told her dad. "I can stay with the Dellachios and go to school every day you are gone."

"You have lots of time for school, Cheeri Biri Bin," Ernie answered. "We are going to climb up and see the sun! You spend any more time with those Italians you'll forget who you are."

She told her father she didn't feel well. But Ernie just put his hand on her forehead to feel for fever. He shook his head and told her that she "…just had the pip."

72

"Child o' mine," he said, "If you are too sick to hunt with me and Uncle Billy and Tom, you are too sick to go to school."

She saw his logic. Yes, school would keep.

The next morning, they were up before dawn. The horses hitched up easy. The two of them drove east through the cold misty fog toward the mountains. She felt better. It was cold but she had a blanket wrapped around her and wool socks on her feet. Ernie was singing softly as Sarah Ellen watched the light come to the ranches and farms that they passed. She watched for trucks and automobiles. She wished her dad would get an auto and drive her to school in fine style.

Four of the children in her class had either an auto or a truck from Mr. Ford. She knew Mr. Packard made autos too. They didn't leave poop everywhere and she knew that had to be a fine thing for the world. The cool winter daylight made the road ahead of them grow brighter and as they traveled east the fog began to fade. Her father had a pretty little rifle he'd bought from a man down at La Vina store. She wondered if he'd let her shoot it on his trip. He wouldn't let her shoot his shotgun, and his big rifle was too heavy. She never could hold it steady. Uncle Billy had a lighter rifle, and with it she was a good shot. Better than her dad. But then, she could see better because both her eyes worked.

It was dark by the time they got to Uncle Billy's cabin. Mrs. Billy came out to the porch and took Sarah Ellen inside. Mrs. Billy gave her a supper of sour berry mush while the men outside roasted rabbit. The dried berries made the mush tangy and good and the little girl usually liked them, but this night the berries made her mouth hurt. She didn't eat much, but rolled out her bedding where she usually slept over by the woodstove and went to sleep.

In the morning Uncle Billy, Tom and another man Sarah had never met packed the horses and began the long trek to the deer grounds. The other man, Solo, used a different kind of knot when he cinched up the pack animals. Tom told her Solo was a Mono, not Chukchansi and they did things differently. Mrs. Billy had given her a little bag of jerky and she had her canteen full of mountain water. Walking beside the horses, she felt better.

When the sun was high they stopped and she could look down and see the lake on top of Crane Valley. They ate lunch, made coffee and rested awhile. Sarah Ellen wanted to go to sleep, but it was time to go on. The trail got steeper and now and then one of the horses would misstep and make a clunky noise as its hoof would slip on a rock or some gravel. It was warmer, and she took off her jacket. Late in the afternoon her headache came back. But it was just the pip, so she didn't say anything.

They didn't see one deer all day. No scat either. In the evening the men took turns singing. Tom and Solo tried to out do each other with their Indian songs and Solo made a soft pounding noise on the back of a frying pan with a chamois over his hand. His drumming made Sarah Ellen wanted to step dance around the campfire as she had other hunting trips, but she was too tired. She cuddled up close to her dad, and he took his turn by singing army songs. The men got quiet.

Ernie sang *Apple Blossom-Time*. Then he put his arm around her and hugged her. He sang her favorite song, *Two Little Girls in Blue*, and Sarah Ellen was happy there in her mother's own mountains listening to her father's songs. She climbed into her bedroll.

She could hear the men talk. Around the fire in the winter night the men talked about setting up a business to pack easterners in to the mountains now that the war was over. No place would give better deer or trout than here. "Better than working lumber," Tom said. "Better than working the ranches," Solo countered.

The next day Sarah Ellen woke up feeling sicker and her headache was back. But she said nothing. That day they climbed higher. She walked slower with her dad while Uncle Billy, Tom and Solo led the horses up the trail ahead of them. Ernie told her how the Chukchansi and the Mono Indians used to be enemies. "See how Tom and Solo are friends? One day the Hun and we Americans will be friends again."

She knew he was talking about the war that was just over. When they were in a stand of white pines they found deer trace. Solo pointed off to the left, and Uncle Billy nodded.

They turned a mile in that direction and then tied up the stock. Tom and Solo went off with their guns, but came back with no kill but a couple of birds. By that time Uncle Billy and Ernie had set up the tent and made a fire. Supper was cooking. That evening Sarah Ellen wasn't hungry and she felt hot.

She went to bed early and didn't even want to listen to the men talk. Her face hurt and her stomach hurt. She could smell her dad's pipe smoke blending its smell with the campfire. She thought she could smell sweet grass burning and hear Uncle Billy praying for a good hunt. She was finally lulled into a restless sleep.

She woke up in the middle of the night aware she was very sick. Then she didn't know anything more until a doctor at the Burnett Sanatorium in Fresno sat down in a chair by her white bed in a white room and told her she was lucky to be alive.

"Those Indian men saved your life, little girl. They forced some kind of Indian tea down your throat and used snow packed in blankets to pull your fever down.

"Why, your father told us that two of those men ran for miles to a mountaintop bring snow down to cool you. You'd had fever fits up at the camp. Once they thought you were dead. The men built a litter and toted you down out of those mountains without stopping to eat or rest themselves."

Sarah Ellen found she'd been in the hospital for two weeks. She asked the nurses what was wrong with her and was told that she'd had the worst case of mumps any of them had ever seen. "Only diphtheria and Spanish flu brings children as near to death as you have been, Dearie," one of the white-capped nurses told her. "It went into brain fever."

 Her dad came in and sat by her bed. He looked sadder than she had ever seen him. "Didn't we get a deer?" she asked him. He just put his head down on the bed and she could see he was crying. Everything in her life changed that winter. The public heath service reported that a little girl, eleven years old, nearly died while camped out in the wild with four men. Affidavits were signed. There was public outrage, and Sarah Ellen was taken from her father's custody.

Sarah Ellen spent the rest of her childhood in a succession of foster homes, for a time when she was in her teens she with an aunt, but then the court intervened again. By that time she had grown used to being called various names: Sarah, Ellen, Mary Ellen, Mary, even Red for the reddish-gold of her hair. She answered to whatever she was called.

 She graduated from Madera High School with honors while living with a Seventh Day Adventist family who knew her father and were very kind to her. She never went hunting again. Nor did she ever eat sour berries or look down from a mountain to see the lake that covered Crane Valley. But Ernie kept his promise to his wife.

Their daughter never forgot who she was. I am her daughter. The first thing she taught me was that I was a Chukchansi child. The second thing she taught me was that everything changes.

***

Madera County
1940

Ernie squinted up his good eye and looked off across the fields. Over on Dominic's land beyond the road, black waves of old burn cut into the barley stubble. The burn ended in a long ditch that separated Dominic's property from the Miller ranch. Fence posts ran jagged along the edge of the far side of the road and long ruts crisscrossed where tires had dug into the dust during the summer. The fire didn't cross the road. On Ernie's land the wild barley had bleached over the summer. It still stood stiff and tall, waiting for Mueller's cows to chew it down. Ernie's other eye saw nothing.

He could scare children with his other eye. Of an afternoon or evening when she and Morris were in from fieldwork, he'd go down to Gussie's and sit out on her porch with Morris and scatter all those damn kids that hung around there. He thought about the kids, how they'd run and hide in the grapevines whenever they saw his rackety car pull up in front of Gussie's place.

That old black woman got so mad at him. Sometimes he turned quickly when he was going on to her porch to make a face at the kids. He'd put his evil eye on them.

Always made him chuckle, but Gussie'd get fluttery mad. Wanted him to get a patch for his eye. What'd he want to go and do that for? It'd get all sweaty and uncomfortable.

He laughed to himself, thinking of Morris and Gussie. They were good friends, though he was about the only white man who came around to sit on their porch.

Over by the pump a child played, and from the chicken house's shade the long tail of a dog poked out into the sunshine. The child was piling up dirt into mounds around the bucket that sat beneath the pump. She filled her hands with dirt and slowly let it seep out between her fingers.

Ernie settled down in the swing and lit his pipe. He watched her play. Wasn't much like her mother. Ellen wouldn't like it, but he let the child run around in her underpants until the mosquitos came out. Nobody around his place to care what she wore on a hot day. Three-year-old kid didn't need pinafores or shoes. He sat in his swing, tasted the tobacco and watched her hug up the dirt and then let it down on the mounds. She straightened up and let the last of what she had in her hands filter out into the green water of the drip bucket.

"Child, you come and get out of that water," the old man called to her. He rocked slowly back and forth.

"I'm not in the water," she answered.

"I know you're not, but Boy and all those kittens drink out of there. Boy don't want to drink dirty water. How'd you like it if I gave you dirty water to drink?"

He heard her mumble something and he said, "You got something to say you'd better say it out clearly."

She looked slanty at him and then yelled, "I'm where I'm 'aposed to be. You leave me alone."

The swing stood under a row of eucalyptus trees that grew on the east side of the yard. Between them and the house was an open area where Ernie left the car when he wasn't going anywhere. A hundred feet behind the house were some outbuildings, a chicken house and a two-seater outhouse. Closer to the house and a bit to the west was a windmill. Between the windmill and the kitchen door stood the pump. He had marked off the area for her. She was free as long as she stayed in the dusty triangle of the house and trees and outbuildings.

"Now you just behave yourself, or I'll put you over in the chicken yard, and the chickens will peck your feet good."

She turned her back on him and didn't sass him anymore. He leaned his head back and was glad he had trees to put his swing under. Gussie and Morris didn't have one tree around that old shack of theirs. It just jutted out of the vineyard with no shade. 'Course the Italians always had plenty shade around them. Soon he'd get himself some pomegranates from Lidio and Mary Lou. Always get pomegranates from the Italians.

The girl got up and walked over to the swing. The old man watched her come up near him. She reached out her hand and rubbed it across the green and orange stripes of the cushions. She took both hands and began pushing the cushions until the swing was rocking.   After a long time she said, "Grandpa, when's my mommy coming back?"

The old man took his pipe out of his mouth and spat onto the dirt by his feet. Then he reached out and tried to pull her up into the swing beside him, but she backed away. "Your mommy's got to tend to her business. She'll be back soon's she can."

"She promised."

"Your mommy lived here when she was a little girl like you." He remembered all the years. It wasn't so different. Except electricity was in past the Miller place now. He could have hooked into it but there was no need. "She played under these trees. When she got big enough she went down the road to La Vina School." He closed his good eye and said, "Little girl, your grandma planted these trees nearly thirty years ago in 1911. They weren't so big then."

82

"Don't talk to me," she whispered.

But he kept on talking until she ran away from the swing. She ran past the car and past the stump where he killed chickens, past the long row of trees. She ran down the dusty drive toward the road. The old man watched her go, and then he got up and followed.

She dropped into the ditch that separated his forty acres from the road. He stood on the culvert crossing at the edge of the ditch and looked down at her. Sunlight filled up half the ditch and glinted the quartz sand that marked where the water had been last time it ran. Now the weeds growing up the sides of the ditch were old and prickly. The child slid to the bottom of the ditch and put her hands into the warm sand.

"Rattlesnakes will get you down in that ditch." Ernie stood and looked down at her and he was smiling. "You climb on out of there." His voice was soft and slow. He pronounced that last word, they-ya.

"No."

"Come on."

"No." She wouldn't look at him.

"Come on you get out of there. If you're a good girl, I'll take you hunting with me."

'When?"

"Tonight."

"You promise?"

"Yep."

She climbed up the side of the ditch, and they walked back to the house and went inside. He took a pot of cold coffee from the top of the woodstove and poured some out into a mug and used the hand pump at the sink to draw a glass of water for her.

"I want coffee too," she said.

Ernie nodded at her and poured a swish of dark liquid into her glass. The coffee swirled down making a pale amber spiral in the water. He put the pot back on thetop of the stove and sat down beside her at the kitchen table. He pushed a small plate of leftover biscuits across the linoleum strip covering the table. She picked one up and dunked it in the glass. Ernie reached to the shelf above the table and got down a deck of cards. The old man laid out solitaire. She watched him for a little while, smugly drank her coffee, and then went outside to call the dog and share what was left of a second biscuit.

The old man went outside. It was mid-afternoon. The heat was glaring off the buildings and making their unpainted sides smell sweetish and rotting. The place was his and he took pleasure that it was aging along with him. He didn't plant anything. Things grew, cottontails, wild barley, field mice and horny toads, touch-me-nots and yellow poppies in season. But on his place the things that grew did it of themselves.

Ernie didn't plow the soil. Gussie tried to talk him into planting the forty acres to cotton to make a profit, but he was independent. He didn't need to do that. Surgeons in Jacksonville during the Spanish-American War had given him a blind eye and a lifetime of headaches while treating him for brain fever. It bought him an army pension. The check every month paid for his beans, coffee and taxes. He could look out across his land and know it was his.

Boy whined and thumped his tail against the rough boards of the chicken house. Ernie scanned slowly past the windmill and saw a shape coming diagonally across the fields toward the house. The old man kept watching. The child saw him and went back into the house. Pretty soon Ernie could make out a man's checkered shirt and his rifle swinging and waved to Dos, and then Ernie went to sit in the swing out of the sun. Dos' right arm
stopped at the elbow and his shirt was pinned up. But he could shoot pretty well. Better'n anyone would have thought.

The ground beneath the swing was littered with small dry eucalyptus horns. The day before the girl had made little pyramids of the small hard bits of debris from the trees. They formed an irregular circle of mounds around the base of one of the trees.

As Dos slid his gun under the barbed wire and spread the wire to step through, Boy came out and loped over to the swing where Ernie sat. The dog went slowly around the swing, circled and lay down, resting his head on one of the eucalyptus mounds.

Frank Doster crossed the yard. He bent down and put his gun on the ground again, and then squatted down beside it. He managed to take a pack of cigarettes from his shirt pocket and light up with one hand without losing his balance.

"Lidio got hisself in jail again." Doster was a young man, but he cackled out the words like an old crone or the squabbling poultry.

The old man looked at him but didn't answer. "You got any money?" Dos asked.

The old man shook his head no.

"Goddam, Ernie. We got to get him out."

The old man took his time answering. "Why?" he said. "We didn't put him in."

"Well, shit, Ernie. We only need thirty bucks more an' we can get him out." Dos picked up some of the dry eucalyptus horns and tossed them under the canvas fringe of the swing to wake the dog.

The old man frowned at Doster's raw language, but it was a free country. "What's he done this time?"

"That damn Lee-dee-o got in a fight with Mary Lou down 't the Italian store and Gina called the deputy. Can you beat that? She's Lee's cousin, and she called the law on him. Jackson was just outside gassing up and she went and hollered him into the store. Dos grinned and rubbed his jaw, "Jackson cuffed him and got him on drunk and disorderly.

Damn fool of a Lee got no sense. Mary Lou aggravates him and he rises to her bait. Now she says they can just keep him. She don't care. Gina swore out the complaint because Lee knocked over a four-shelf display of Acme. Broke every bottle. Hell, Ernie, dove season'll be here and gone unless we get him out."

Ernie started to answer, but the screen door on the kitchen banged and interrupted his thinking. No one came out. He looked up toward the house and the screen door banged again, and then again.

87

"What you got in your house?"

"Little girl's here."

"I remember. You tole me she'd be here for a couple weeks. Why'd your girl bring the kid up here? She so busy down L.A. she can't take care of her own kid?"

"She was married over in Yuma this week past. They need time to get settled down."

"Who's she marry this time?" Dos reached over and pulled his rifle and moved it closer to him. The kid might come out of the house, think it was a toy.

"The Hungarian. You remember. She brought him up here last spring. They stayed a couple of days. Fished. Took some salmon out of the San Joaquin."

"Marryin' that ol' furr-i-ner?" Dos looked surprised and then smiled. "Hell, Ernie, that girl of yours could 'a stayed round here and married a Mex. She din't need to go down to L.A to find som'un couldn't speak English right. He's near as old as you."

Ernie just looked off across the yard and fields for a while and then he said, "He's a good man. He's done all right for himself. She's better off with him than a ragged five acre Okie."

"You're sumthin' better, old man?"

"I'm not a ragtag, uneducated, one-armed dustbowl Okie."

The two men laughed together for a time and then the screen door began banging again. The old man stood up and took a big handkerchief out of the pocket of his overalls. He wiped the moisture that had collected around his blind eye and put the handkerchief back into his pocket.

Dos got up too, slower, and moving almost sullenly. He began walking across the yard. "Be back by tomorrow morning, for it gets too hot. See if you can figger out how we can get Lee out. Only need thirty dollars, Ernie." He stopped for a moment and added, "We gonna need your car too. Morris says he needs a new clutch afore his truck'll go anywhere. We get the money, you can driver us to town to bail Lee out."

Ernie nodded. "See what I can do." Lee was always ready to lend a hand. Mechanical. Couldn't have replaced the shaft on the windmill last winter without Lee. He owed him thirty dollars for his helpfulness. The old man gave a gesture with his hand and a little tuck of his head to let Dos know he was in agreement. Doster started across the fields.

The girl in the house was lying on the cool linoleum, using her feet on the door. Ernie didn't clean her up for supper until the sun was low. He helped her wash, get her blouse and overalls on, and buckled her sandals. It was too hot to cook, so they ate cold canned beans and thick slices of salami with muscat grapes. He didn't make fresh coffee. He poured cold bitter liquid left from the noon meal into his mug and put some for her in a china cup he'd half filled with canned milk. He added a little water and let her stir a spoon of sugar in the mix. After they ate, he rinsed the dishes off by the pump at the sink.

The girl went back outside and ran to the swing. Through the screen he watched her jump up into it and rock back and forth while he cleaned up. Boy curled beneath her. She reached down to pet him and fell out.

It was getting dim in the kitchen. Ernie reached up behind the stovepipe and pulled out a little tin box. Inside there were five ten-dollar bills. He put three of them in his wallet and then put the two remaining bills back into the box and stuck it back into its place. The old man counted out the money in his wallet and it came to thirty-one dollars and sixty-seven cents. He put the wallet back into the pocket of his overalls, lit the kerosene lamp and put it on the table. The kerosene's smell drove out the night smells of wild barley and eucalyptus that were coming through the screen door. He decided to get makings for corn bread set out for the next morning.

90

The girl came running to the door. She stood there watching him from the other side of the screen. The lamplight was bright in her eyes and the old man smiled at her but she didn't smile back.

"Better come in, now, honeybee," he said.

"You promised. It's night now."

He winked his good eye at her and said, "You go up by the car. I'll be 'long pretty soon. Got to do my chores yet."

Ernie watched her run to the car. She couldn't open the door, so she sat on the running board. He finished in the kitchen. This was a time of day he liked. The sun was all gone, but for a pale streak just above the West Side's hills, and the chickens were settling down. If he remembered to listen each night, just about now a cool west breeze would come up rustling through the eucalyptus as it tempered the day's heat.

He hooked the wire door to the chicken yard against coyotes and drew the calf to the barn with some of the chicken grain. He dropped the latch beam securely. Then went back to the house. He counted the eggs in the bowl on the shelf above the table. There were nineteen. Tomorrow he'd stop by Gina's and he'd trade eggs for produce. He turned down the lamp and went outside. A couple of gunnysacks lay in a pile by the back steps and he reached down and picked one up. Throwing it over his arm, he started for the car.

The girl said, "You forgot your gun."

"I don't need a gun, honey."

"You made me wait too long and big ol' giant mosquitos came and bit me."

He turned toward her and said, "Let me see."
But she pulled away from him and frowned. "What are we going to hunt?"

The old man pushed in the clutch and threw the car into reverse. The little girl fell against him as the car jerked back down the long dirt drive toward the road. As the car bumped across the wooden boards over the ditch culvert, she straightened up enough to see out the windows and said, "You forgot to turn on the lights."

He snapped on the switch and one lone headlight shone out from the old ford toward the house. The car backed onto the road. He straightened out the wheel and headed south toward the river. The last green streak of sky had gone black.

"What are we going to hunt?" she asked again, and her voice was impatient.

The old man looked down at her and said, "We going to get some food for Boy 'cause he's an old dog and can't get it for himself." Then he pushed down on the accelerator until the car hit thirty. They were going fast. Crickets were chirping in the night black ditches on either side of the road. They went faster. For a few miles they saw no other cars and the lights on ranch houses came in view and disappeared quickly. Then in the darkness Ernie could smell riverweeds over the smell of alfalfa.

Ernie began to sing a song he taught her called *Standing on the Promises*. The car was going so fast it was shivering. Bugs smashed themselves against the window of the car. Way off ahead of them something flashed across the road. Then, just behind it a rabbit froze, blinded by the one white light of the old rackety car.

The old man swerved the car and the car raced toward the animal. There was a thud. Ernie hit the brake and the car skidded to a stop. He cranked the car into reverse and backed up. He turned off the engine and put his pipe up on the dashboard. He reached down on the floor on the passenger side, grabbed up the gunnysack, and got out.

The girl watched him through the open door of the car, and then knelt high enough on the seat to watch through the windshield.

Ernie walked forward into the white light of the headlight. He bent down and picked up the quivering rabbit by its hind feet and it hung still. Pink coils slipped down from its belly. With his free hand he worked the mouth of the sack open and, when it was opened wide enough, he dropped the dead animal into it. Then he wiped his hands on a kerchief and took up the sack and went back in the car.

She scooted over to make room for him, and he dropped the sack down on the floor below her. She pulled her feet up on the seat. They went on singing the old hymns he'd taught her, *Rock of Ages*, *Peace in the Valley*, *Take My Hand, Precious Lord*, and she remembered most of the words. They got two more rabbits that night.

The night closed in all around them. They drove home slowly. She wiggled closer to her grandfather, and he put his arm around her. He was a one-eyed man in an ol' one-eyed Ford, and he could drive with one arm just fine. He began singing, "Bye baby bunting, Grandpa's gone a-hunting, to fetch a little rabbit skin, to wrap his baby bunting in."

"I'm not a baby."

"Tomorrow we'll go to town for ice cream."

"You promise?"

"Yep. First, we'll go to the courthouse."

"What's a cordhouse?"

***

95

~~~<O>~~~

Guns and Roses

When I was a wee tiny girl, three or four times a year my mother would take my baby sister and me up into the Central Valley. We would drive a long way from our apartment building in Culver City. We would go into what I knew as rich people's country, to my mother's aunt's home in Fresno.

Auntie had a house on East Thesta Street. It was the prettiest house I'd ever been in. My great aunt, the daughter of a cowboy and a Chukchansi Indian woman, had had the good fortune of being born beautiful. Although her early life was tragic, she survived. She married white and, the second time, she married well.

One afternoon I was sitting on the cool cement of the bungalow porch just watching the street. I could hear my mother and great aunt's voices come through the window. I liked to listen to my mother when she was talking especially if she didn't know I was there. I could hear Auntie trying to persuade my mother to come with her on a hunting trip over on the West Side. I knew that "the West Side" meant the Coast Range hills. Though I couldn't yet read, my mother had taught me the landscape of her own years and I knew the valley and the names of its surrounding mountains as well as I knew our apartment was on Venice Boulevard near Bagley Avenue.

"Only be gone four or five days. Charlie can't get off work," Auntie said, "but he can get the truck to drive us an' come pick us up. Sister and I'll get two bucks sure. If you come, might be three or four."

Charlie was a relative Auntie talked about a lot. But I didn't know him. Charlie shot mountain lions for the government.

I wanted my mother to say "Yes", but she didn't. I kept as quiet as they talked about guns and shells and shot, I thought maybe I could go along if my mother would just say "Yes". I wanted to meet an uncle who shot mountain lions. I wanted to climb on trails and shoot a deer.

There was a picture of my great aunt and her sister with their rifles in the room where my sister and I slept. In the picture my great aunts wore shirts and pants like men, and high boots. At their feet were four antlered deer, heads lolled all twisted over and eyes wide open. The deer in the picture were my introduction to what it was to be dead. It seemed a very natural thing. My mother had taken me to a theater to see *Gone With The Wind*, but I hadn't seen *Bambi*. My consciousness had not yet been raised by cartoons.

My mother told me that the women of my family, my mother, Auntie and Auntie's sister, were Indians and we were not like other women. We did what we wanted. Observation had taught me that this was true. The women we knew had no children. In our building women played a card game called 'bridge' and drank cocktails on long, sleepy afternoons while their husbands were at work. Playing cards all afternoon seemed a very dull thing to do. I'd gone with my mother when she was invited to a neighbor's apartment. We didn't stay long. Mother didn't like cocktails and she thought playing cards was dull too.

I liked that Auntie and her sister and my mother were women who took sage and salt, knives and rifles and went hunting wearing shirts and pants like men.

Auntie continued to coax my mother to come along on the west side. I heard my mother refer to 'little distractions like a pregnancy' and a husband who wouldn't like her 'going off'. I wasn't sure what pregnancy meant, but thought 'going off' was what we were doing when we came by ourselves to visit Auntie.

Hearing disappointment in my mother's voice I knew she wouldn't agree to go.

I wanted to show myself and argue in Auntie's favor. I wanted to wheedle and whine. With the knowledge of a child's power, I thought perhaps I could persuade mother better than Auntie could. But I knew I couldn't say anything. I huddled down below the window even further and kept very still. I'd learned long before that discretion was the price I had to pay for eavesdropping.

99

We didn't get to go to the west side and bring home venison with Auntie and her sister May, my other great aunt. I didn't learn to shoot at a living target, to gut and clean a carcass, or the joy of cooking fresh kill over an open fire.

The fogs of winter settled over the valley. Not until the following spring did my mother drive us back up to the Central Valley. I had a baby brother by then. The nation was at war but I didn't know it. I knew that the roses in my great aunt's yard were gorgeous and huge, and I was happy to be back in Fresno.

In the dining room a bouquet of the roses filled a big blue bowl in the center of the table. We followed Auntie through the house to the kitchen where she made a tea for my mother. Mother sat on a kitchen chair to nurse my brother. My little sister toddled to the pots and pan drawer and began to root around. Disassembled gun parts were scattered on the table and the room was filled with the good strong smell of gun solvent. I asked my aunt if that was the gun she used when she went deer hunting. I know I used a sulky voice. I hadn't forgotten my disappointment from the fall and felt compelled to show it.

She laughed at me. "This is a sawed off shotgun," she said. "Its for snakes, not for deer."

I was flippant and said, "There aren't any snakes here."

100

Auntie smiled at my mother and then turned to say to me, "Now, girl, a woman never knows when there might be a snake on the porch." This made my mother laugh, but I didn't think it very funny.

"Ellen," my great aunt said to my mother as baby brother contentedly sucked away, "you have to teach this girl the difference between her guns. She's near five years old and she don't know a shotgun from a rifle."

Auntie left the room for a minute and came back. She draped a big piece of buckskin across my shoulders from the tan bundle in her arms. It was heavy and soft. My little sister pulled out two pot lids and they clanged on the linoleum. Auntie showed my mother the other, larger, skins she had tanned from the fall hunt. I put a finger through a hole where a bullet had gone through the skin I had around me. I asked what kind of a bullet it was, and my mother said it was a 30-30 just like her rifle used.

I knew Auntie would let me take the deerskin home to keep. The scent of the newly tanned skin was sharp compared to the fragrance of the roses drifting in from the dining room. I was yet to learn that while we were hunters, we were not gatherers. It was Uncle Lou who tended the roses and brought them into the house.

Deer skin and the roses' scent blended with odor of gun solvent in my great aunt's kitchen, and the warm air coming in the windows made the smells drift around.

Auntie's kitchen was a good place to be. Baby Joe fell asleep but mother didn't put him down. My sister Nancy played with the pots and pans. Mother and Auntie talked in low voices all afternoon. Eventually Auntie was finished cleaning the shotgun. She put it away along with her cleaning kit. She washed up and began fixing supper. Her husband came home from work and I knew he was happy to see us.

I was glad that the women of my family weren't like other women.

***

Boys on the Playground

(chapter 8: <u>Acts of Kindness, Acts of Contrition</u>)

Monday night's homework was tucked into our books. At St. Blaise, kids were only excused for a death in the immediate family. Jeannie wasn't in our family anywhere. I'd awakened with a dream about a cactus garden. I was playing with cats and dogs in the dream. Then I was flying over the garden with some birds. After I woke up, I remembered everything true and wished I could go back to the dream. We had breakfast and put our uniforms on.

Beth and I were both quiet on the bus. Pretty soon she nudged me. We gathered up our things and went wobbling down the aisle while the bus rattled to a stop. We jumped down the steps and began walking the remaining blocks to St. Blaise. When we reached the playground Beth waltzed off to the little girls' playground. Delores and Pat O'Hara came running to meet me. Pat had yellow ribbons in her hair. Colored ribbons were all right with our uniforms, but not colored socks, which didn't make sense.

We put our books down and went to watch the studio gate across the street from school. Sister would rather we went to St. Blaise church to make a visit with the Blessed Sacrament than watch the actors' gate if we had time before school. We liked watching the actors come in. The people we watched at the gate weren't important. They were just were extras, not movie stars, but they were actors and got paid. Some days, they wore costumes so we could tell what kind of movie the studio was making. We clustered at the fence. I squinted so I could see what the extras were wearing better. The men were wearing slinky jeans and wore cowboy hats and boots; the women wore saloon girl dresses. Some extras smiled and winked at us.

The bell rang. We ran and got in line. In Bungalow Five, Sister Mary Immaculata led our room's prayers, and

the morning filled with lessons. I tried hard to put Jeannie out of my mind, but I kept thinking of how people feel when they think they are going to be killed. She must have had that feeling before she really was killed.

At recess, my friends and I ran between the rectory and Bungalow Six. We were going to act out a western. Delores wanted to be the sheriff, but Kathleen did too. Delores let her, although the game was Delores's idea. The rest of us picked our parts, except for Anna Rose. She didn't want to play if she couldn't be the saloon girl. Pat O'Hara had already dibbed that part. Anna Rose left us to huddle by the hopscotch game. Pretty soon she came back.

Three boys from our class came and stood at the yellow line that separated the girls' from the boys' sides of the asphalt. They were calling me. I ignored them. One of the boys calling me was Paul who knew more about movies than anyone in fifth grade because he was an actor. He might want to tell us something about real westerns for our game. I still ignored them until Andrew McGonigal, the smartest boy in fifth grade, yelled, "Lynn! C'mere, Lynn!"

Andrew and Paul were nice. Tommy was with them, though. He got in bad trouble at school in third grade because Sister heard him making fun of Carol Pistoresi's and my last names. He turned them into bad words. I didn't want to talk to him. I looked at Andrew and Paul.

"Did you know the woman who was murdered up where you live?" Andrew asked.

"She wasn't murdered where I live. She was murdered somewhere else."

"Okay. Maybe. But she lived up there right near you," Tommy Delaney jeered, butting in. Tommy's father was a plumber and he rode with his dad in summer and on holidays. He knew where everyone in our class lived. "So, did you know her?" Tommy yelled at me.

105

This was school, not home. My parents wouldn't know what I did or what I said. It wasn't exactly lying unless they asked me. I nodded my head.

Tommy ducked behind the other two boys and hit at them. "Told you!" he jeered at the boys. "Told you. Told

you."

Paul and Andrew looked surprised. "Did you really?" Paul asked.

Knowing I was breaking my promise to my parents, I answered. "She was my brother's babysitter."

I was telling a kind of lie. Jeannie was Stevie's babysitter if our mother had to go to the doctor or the beauty parlor. But if Beth and I were out of school, and Elsa wasn't there, Jeannie was our babysitter too. It was fun going over to Jeannie's. Once she played monopoly with us. Stevie couldn't yet read the board or cards, and he didn't trust Beth and me not to cheat him. Jeannie helped him. He liked her better than he liked us.

Tommy came circling around in front of Andrew and Paul and his eyes were mean. He almost lunged over the yellow line dividing the playground. "She wasn't a babysitter," he taunted. "She was a whore! Just like the Black Dahlia!" He spun his basketball in the air and caught it. "My dad and mom both said so."

I didn't know the word "whore," but I'd seen it chalked on the sidewalk at the bus stop with other bad words. It was the word he'd turned Horvath into in third grade. "No, she wasn't. She was a nurse. And she was nice." My eyes stung.

"Nope. She was a rotten slut." Tommy bounced the ball up and down as hard and he could while singing, "Your babysitter was a whore, a whore, a whore. A whore, a whore, a whore." I thought he was going to sing it a million times.

Tommy bounced the ball wrong. It arced away. Paul ran and caught it and came back, but he stood away from Tommy and me. Andrew had moved farther away from Tommy too. They looked embarrassed. I just stood there, silent and stupid. I knew what a slut was. Kathleen told the rest of us girls a slut was a woman who hung around guys and got naked and let them touch her body. Jeannie never would be like that.

"I think it's true," Andrew said as kindly as he could. "My parents said her husband killed her because she was running around with men." Andrew was an altar boy. I didn't think he'd lie.

My throat felt tight. But I didn't cry. She wouldn't have done that, and Frank wouldn't have killed her. I couldn't look at Andrew.

Paul moved down toward Bungalow Five, but he was watching and listening. Tommy yelled at Paul to throw the ball back. Paul didn't. I turned and ran as far from the yellow line as I could. I ran to the fence on the other side of the bungalows. The bell was ringing. I knew I'd never speak to Tommy Delaney again in my whole life.

***

In the Sierra, 1856

(from the novel: *EAST OF THE GREAT VALLEY*)

She was guilty of a vanity, and she knew that vanity robbed virtue. Mrs. Simmons had often righteously quipped, "One is never so low that there is no one below to pity, or never so high that there is no one above to envy." She had taken it to heart. Yet Nancy would rather her place be on the high side. As soon as she saw the West's rugged beauty, its mountain peaks and quick-running streams she recognized its promise. She lived higher here than Indiana's citizens could dream. And the height was in more than just a matter of California's mountain geography.

The pup scratched at the back door and that brought her out of her reminiscence and back to the present. The men said that there were no wolves in this part of the world. She didn't believe them, in spite of what she'd told her son. The ragged limping Indian who was setting posts down at Mr. Dickey's store told the boys that there were greys roaming in the tall pines between the mining camps and this valley.

The Indian's English was poor, but she and the boys understood him. The man pointed to the northeastern hills and unhitched a wolf tail he'd strung on some kind of thready twine around his waist and let them hold it.

Her boys petted it and traded it among them. It seemed that old man was trying to claim that the wolf tail held some kind of magic. Frederick, loading the wagon, took notice. He turned, strode over and grabbed the tail out of Tom's hands, and tossed it back at the old man.

If the wolves were gone, the Indians were practically gone. Mr. Dickey told her that the miners in the valley had near wiped them out and burnt their villages before her family arrived. It was sport to shoot at them if they walked on the roads. Her husband knew this, and it bothered her to realize that what had been done gave him no bad feelings. Mrs. Barrow who lived miles up the creek told her they used Mono Indians to dig wells and ditches and to lay fence.

"They'll work for a little food," she'd said. "Ranchers hire so as not to pay in money." But Frederick wouldn't.

Mr. Dickey told her there were some Indian women and a few children left. "They live in little dens up in the mountains like the bears. If we aren't killing them outright, we seem to bring them our sicknesses, alcohol is a poison for them."

She thought of the Reverend Simmons' sermons. "I think that is pitiful, Mr. Dickey," she said. "But alcohol is poisonous to white people too, I think."

"As I do, Mrs. McCreary."

Mr. Dickey took a fancy to Indians and told the primitives which ranches along Crane Valley and the Waukeen River would give them work and not run them off. He gave them old tools and discarded items he came by. Nancy appreciated that. Leviticus 23:22 admonished that gleanings be left for the poor. Homeless, sick Indians were certainly poor. She liked Mr. Dickey. So, after Frederick's mother died, worn out from the long trek, she thought long on how clothes could be similar to gleanings.

Nancy bundled up all her mother-in-law's shawls and dresses that had skirts too worn for her to take apart to turn into shirts for the boys. She took the bundle to Mr. Dickey for the Indians. When Frederick finished loading feed grain sacks, he walked in the store for tobacco and saw what she was doing. He didn't interfere, but out in the wagon on their way back to the ranch, he grew upset enough to chastise her in front of the children.

"We're meant to help the godly poor, not give encouragement to idolatrous heathens. I'd rather you burn my mother's clothing than let it touch an Indian's filthy skin," he barked at her. "You could've found some needy Christian woman to dispose of it."

The community of Crane Valley had few women she thought, Christian or otherwise. None were rich, but all would have taken insult from an offer of his mother's old clothing. She ground her teeth at Frederick's meanness, but bowed her head and swallowed down what she wanted to say to him.

The Bible also bound a wife to honor and obey her husband.

***

Ghosts

(from ILSA ROHE
the journalist's interview with Anna)

10 March 1845, Monday afternoon

Da insisted we start at Dry Creek School as soon as we moved here. I try to keep things in order when I tell you how everything happened, but I don't always remember the order. I apologize for that, Mr. Laughton. It was February of 1842 and it was very cold when we started school here. Our Mother Fiona had been dead just over a month. I was eleven and Josiah was six. Andrew was nearly three. Libby had graduated from eighth grade the June before.

When Josie and I went to school here, Andrew cried. He was still a little boy and it was hard for him to see us leave him behind. He had Libby and the wee baby, and our new housemaid, for company. Gran was across the street and coming in and out all the time, but it wasn't the same and he missed us. With our mother's death and then the move, we had missed school often, and he'd grown used to our company. We knew he was confused by so much as had happened. Gran assured Josie and me that Andrew would adjust to our being away, and not to mind his tears. He would get to go to school in his turn.

We first met Mr. Herbert at Dry Creek School. He was very kind and welcoming. Mr. Higgins drove the wagon team that picked us up for school and brought us back home. Perhaps you have met Mr. Higgins? Mr. Higgins is the custodian of the school property. Mr. Higgins is very old, almost as old as Johnnie Reid and older than Gran Da. But he is ever busy, never cranky, and always working for our school.

You haven't yet? Well now, if you are staying with Mr. Herbert while you are in Ohio, you will surely meet him. Dry Creek School was built on land he donated, and it is only a short walk from Mr. Herbert's house. That house where you stay was Mr. Higgins farmhouse once, but he gives its use free to the schoolmaster of Dry Creek School. We wouldn't have a school if he hadn't given the land. He built a small house behind his farmhouse and moved into it, so that the farmhouse proper would be an enticement for a teacher to come to Anderson Township. That was a very good idea, for Mr. Herbert makes extra money over what the township pays him for teaching by renting the extra rooms.

I'm sure you know that Mr. Herbert rents out rooms in the house. Constable Davies is one of the men who live there so you may have seen him. I'm not eager to see him if I go back to school. I hope if I go back to school that he will always be away working in town, and I will never see him. I never want him to ask me any questions again.

Please don't write this down, but Constable Davies is a rough and impatient man. I would be so harsh as to say he is cruel and rude. You should watch out for him. You probably don't have such men in Boston. I'm happy to talk about Mr. Higgins who is good and kind to everyone. If Mr. Herbert didn't tell you, you might think that Mr. Higgins is merely our janitor and driver, and not take notice of him. But you should know he is a very important man in Anderson Township for all that he looks humble.

Mr. Higgins' little house is only the size of a worker's cabin, but he told Josie, Jacob, and me that he liked it better than his old house. He said his old house was filled with the ghosts of those who had passed on. Somehow, that idea of Mr. Higgins' ghosts made me miss my old house more. I think I'd like the ghosts of my mother and Harriet around me, but Gran tells me that the living must stay with the living. She says that ghosts are never good. I disbelieve her. I think ghosts can be good dead if they were good alive.

Oh, Mr. Laughton, I can see from your face that you agree with Gran. It is no matter. Our old house in Iwahata Township belongs to other people now. I can never go back there to visit my mother and Harriet. Though I want to, and I would if I could.

Mr. Higgins does not get pay to drive the four-horse schoolhouse wagon team to pick up those of us who live far down Clark Road. He does it because he likes us and wants us to be educated. Gran says he never had proper schooling and always felt poorer for its lack, though he was a very successful farmer and is not at all poor now. Mr. Herbert drives the smaller wagon to pick up the children far down Dry Creek Road. Our old schoolmaster in Iwahata never cared how we might get to and from school. I think he was happier when we students stayed home because of bad weather and glad when the distance was too great for small children to attend on their own. He wouldn't have to bother with little ones then.

In Iwahata, Da would ride us to school on his horse or he'd drive our carriage, if the weather was poor. But not all families were able to do that. He told us to appreciate that Mr. Herbert and Mr. Higgins are very good to us and treat them with not only respect, but gratitude. Excuse me, Mr. Laughton. I know this isn't what you'd hoped I'd be telling you. The school has nothing to do with what happened at all. But I'm supposed to go back to school before the first of April. It frightens me a little to think of leaving here. Some of the students may ask me questions and stare or look at me oddly. If you don't mind, I think talking about school will help me become accustomed to the idea of it. That's all right, isn't it?

Thank you. I think this is enough for today. I'll see you on Wednesday. I don't want to be disagreeable, but to be truthful, I think you and Gran are wrong about ghosts.

***

116

SR/1991 physical geography - contour mapping

Publication Credits

Page 7   **Under Coyote's Moon**
              "News from Native California," Lindsie Bear,
              editor,   Vol.26 No.4, summer 2013, p.33

Page 13   **Shapeshifters**
              Sierra Wonders, Karen Kimball, editor, The Arts
              Alliance of Three Rivers, California, 2013, p. 18

Page 23   **Oak Trees**
              "Dry Crik Journal," John Dofflemyer, editor, Vol.
              VI, 2010, www.drycrikjournal.org

              Leaves from the Valley Oak, Mary Benton &
              Gloria Getman, editors, 2011, p. 86

Page 24   **Roundelay for Ghost Singers**
              Leaves from the Valley Oak, Mary Benton &
Gloria   Getman, editors, 2011, p. 92

Page 25   **Art Theft**
              Leaves from the Valley Oak, Mary Benton &
Gloria   Getman, editors, 2011, p. 85

Page 26   **The Seagulls' Banquet**
              Leaves from the Valley Oak, Mary Benton &
Gloria   Getman, editors, 2011, p. 87

Page 28   **Conversation**
              "News from Native California," Margaret Dubin,
              editor, Vol.12 No.1, fall 1998, p.31

Page 29   **Tribal Identity Grade Three**
              "News from Native California," Margaret
              Dubin,   editor, Vol.12 No.1, fall 1998, p.30

Page 46   *Matrilineage*
           The Dirt Is Red Here,
           Margaret Dubin, editor, Heyday, Berkeley,
           California, 2002, p.49

Page 48   *Marge's shoes*
           "American Life in Poetry," Ted Kooser, ed.
           University of Nebraska, Lincoln, 2016,
           column # 596 (online and print)

           Red Indian Road West, Kurt Schweigman &
           Lucille Lang Day, editors, 2016, Scarlet Tanager
               Books. p. 82

Page 50   *Haswana Wotiye*
           The Dirt Is Red Here , Poet's Invitational
             Presentation, PMLA International Conference,
           San Diego, Dec. 3, 2003

           "News from Native California,"
           Margaret Dubin, editor, Vol.17 No.4,
           2004, p. 17

           "Dry Crik Journal," John Dofflemyer, editor, Vol.
           VI, 2010, www.drycrikjournal.org,

           Red Indian Road West, Kurt Schweigman &
           Lucille Lang Day, editors, 2016, Scarlet Tanager
           Books. p.84

Page 53   *Vertebral Doggerel*
           Leaves from the Valley Oak, Mary Benton &
             Gloria Getman, editors, 2011, p. 97

Page 59   *Winter Beginning, Winter Ending*
           Spring Salmon, Hurry To Me,

121

***

Sample Illustrations from the
Children's Books

LION SINGER

Lion Singer / Sylvia Ross / ISBN 1-59714-009-0
Heyday Books, Berkeley, California

Summary: In long-ago California in the area populated by the
various tribes of the Yokuts group, Dog Cry, a young
Chukchansi Indian boy, saves his little sister from a mountain
lion and gains a new name.

BLUE JAY GIRL

Blue Jay Girl / Sylvia Ross / ISBN 978-1-59714-127-7
Heyday Books, Berkeley, California

Summary: In long-ago California in the area populated by the
various tribes of the Yokuts group, a young Yaudanchi girl
who is troubled because of her impetuous nature turns to the

tribe's shaman for advice on how to be less like a blue jay and more like a quail. The book includes a glossary and facts about the Indians of the Tule River Indian Reservation who descend from a number of Yokuts tribes including the Yaudanchi.

FABLES IN AN OLD STYLE
FÁBULAS EN UN ESTILO ANTIGUO
BOOK ONE Sylvia Ross/ ISBN 978-0-578-16866-1
Bentley Avenue Books, Lemon Cove, California

FABLES IN AN OLD STYLE
FÁBULAS EN UN ESTILO ANTIGUO
BOOK TWO Sylvia Ross/ ISBN 978-0-692-52507-4
Bentley Avenue Books, Lemon Cove, California

in order of publication:

*LION SINGER (2005)

*BLUE JAY GIRL (2008)

ACORNS AND ABALONE (2011, expanded version 2017)

ACTS OF KINDNESS, ACTS OF CONTRITION (2011)

EAST OF THE GREAT VALLEY (2012)

ILSA ROHE (2014)

*FABLES IN AN OLD STYLE
   FÁBULAS EN UN ESTILO ANTIGUO (2015)

COMING TO COMPLETION (2017)

* for children

Made in the USA
Monee, IL
06 August 2021

74891386R00075